REHUMANIZE ME

**an anthology of Black youth voices
by students from Minneapolis**

a publication by 826 MSP

ISBN 13: 978-1-63489-552-1

Library of Congress Catalog Number has been applied for.
Printed in the United States of America
First Printing: 2022

26 25 24 23 22   5 4 3 2 1

Cover design by Myc Dazzle
Interior design by Patrick Maloney

Wise Ink Creative Publishing
807 Broadway St. NE
Suite 46
Minneapolis, MN 55413

All that you touch
You Change.
All that you Change
Changes you.
The only lasting truth
Is Change.

Octavia E. Butler, *Parable of the Sower*

Contents

This symbol indicates a potential trigger warning
due to the piece's content.

Foreword from the Student Editorial Board

As we looked back on bringing this book together, it was challenging to put our thoughts and experiences into words—especially as we were navigating and discovering who we are as individuals and finding ourselves and what's important to us. But we continued and discovered what's true for each of us, and it felt natural to write about it and what matters. Making this book was one of the trials that refined us because of the challenges that we had to endure to get here. We consider ourselves writers now because we have been featured in this book. This project was motivating because we got to work with amazing writers, and that's how we got our passion for writing.

And really, this book feels pretty big! Outside of all the things we do, art is one of the things that matters to us the most. Having a group of people who are peers that are passionate about poetry and writing is really inspiring and keeps us working on our craft. Each of us has made some kind of art before—drawing, making music on Soundcloud, other kinds of writing—but to actually be published, to go through the process, makes us want to learn more about ownership and how to grow our art, music, and writing. To us, a writer or an artist is someone who inspires and makes a mark on the world in any way they can. We hope other students in the city see our work and are inspired to tap into their own inner writer and artist. We hope this book connects with them, that they see themselves in our writing, and that it inspires them to do the same.

Rehumanize Me doesn't just capture the Black experience in the way society and media depict it. This experience is not just about the pain and the oppression, but also about joy and laughter. *Rehumanize*

Me literally does just that. It rehumanizes us. It's a book that has helped us remember—and, we think, will help others remember— that Black people aren't just a political subject. We dance and paint and take care of plants and make movies too. We love. We are just as deserving of a human experience.

For us as youth of color in our community, we can help other youth that are looking for experiences and opportunities to write and have their voices be in the conversation. To express some sort of release of all that they are feeling when it comes to these systems of oppression. Systems of oppression that beat up on us every day. We hope this book can bring peace or some sort of healing or closure of one chapter of somebody's life, or a sense of relatability or comfort. Especially the comfort of knowing that there are other people that you may not know, but they have their story that you can relate to. And that's something amazing.

One thing people should take away after reading this book is hearing—not just reading, but understanding—the stories of the students and what they have to share. See that the youth's voices have been suppressed and that it's finally time for them to make their voices heard. They also should take away the stories and relate them to themselves, learn from them, and—hopefully—use the stories to educate and teach others. They should read to be responsive instead of reactionary. Especially non-Black people. People should also leave this book questioning the unconscious biases that they have not only towards Black people but towards other people impacted by oppression.

People should buy this book because they can get a better grasp into the young minds of Black youth. We have been silenced for way too long, and now that we are speaking, it is our time to be heard and your time to listen. Each page records our soul, our truth, and our being—unapologetically. To be Black was seen as unlucky or undesirable, but we are reclaiming it to be a beautiful thing. Because to be Black was always beautiful. This book is me, it's you, it's us.

"Write to discover" is our challenge to you as readers of this book.

Signed,

The Young Authors' Book Project Student Editorial Board

Hawi Emeru
Haney Mohamed
Fredrick Emdin
Yahanna
Elsie Carmona Quiterio
Bezawit Abate
Salma Khalif

Joy

By Fredrick Emdin

This is that fresh air you breathe in
Every first day of your favorite seasons
Got the trees around you changin'
And your routines keep going
You see that you're growing
And loving,
And loving
Your skin melanin and that beautiful full grin
While the sun rises from the east and beams like teeth
I arise to my feet and feel every breeze
Warm, Cold, my Joy is bold
So bold and soft like the metal of Gold
Sadness can't take something I'll never have sold
My Joy bonded to my soul like a bike locked to a pole

Day to day,
Yes
I know that my Joy won't grow old

Fredrick Emdin is a freshman at Augsburg University and a recent graduate of South High. He likes Childish Gambino and spitting bars, and aspires to become a doctor. He also makes music on SoundCloud by the name CHIDIMMA.

A Letter to You

By Elsie Carmona Quiterio

Take your bothered hands and cut them off.

Take your story and put it in the pit with the others.

We are not the God of undeserving or un-reserving.

Touch all your Body and count your organs. We're not going to war.
We're fighting battles that will take, but also make our bodies.

It will drain our blood,
        Our voice,
        Our peace,
        Resurrect me.

Bury my body now if I can't speak.

My Black women. My sisters, my blood. We stand in solidarity as we
are diminished in conversation.

My body aches.

Walking and screaming chants, my mind is jumbled with phrases
and poems that could heal your wounds.

We must breathe.

Black men. Take your glory and hang it on the wall. You deserve it. You served your life to be healed, even a rotten one with as much value as the white man. Peace to your existence.

Take those Black men and take them back to their school days where they were violently caressed and verbally abused by a system that demanded nothing but their failure.

The Public School System didn't feel the need to count colored folk for other than "good statistics."

Our teachers of color feel alone and our students of color feel exposed like an experiment.

Am I alive?

Are we living?

Our ground is built off of our slave brothers.
Our captured mothers.
Our terrified children.

Children don't belong in cages. We are human.
Black brothers don't need racial violence.
Violence is what they breathe, it's what killed them.

Elevate my Words. Hear my Truth. Become a believer of Faith. We are reserving our Future and deconstructing our Past.

Freedom doesn't exist in human regulation.

We renew our Power. We the Youth will claim our right to live off the Promise.

Of a better Future.

Free me from my Trauma, let me sit in my Serenity of Peace.

Elsie Carmona Quiterio is an Afro-Mexican born and raised in Minneapolis, Minnesota. She is involved in Black Student Union, student council, Latinx Club, cheerleading, Blackbox Social Justice Theatre, and Integrate MPS. Elsie helped create a social and racial justice affinity board at Washburn High School that speaks directly with the principal to get BIPOC students involved. Outside of school, she works to heal physical and generational trauma with her community through breath work with Irreducible Grace Foundation, an intergenerational team of healers of color. She is a part of the NAACP youth chapter and participates in a program called Project Diva founded by Neda Kellog. She plans to continue her activism into her college years in 2022.

When Will It End?

By Bezawit Abate

Hi
I'm [ ].
I know you can see that I'm [ ],
But I want you to **know**
That I am [ ].

Oh sorry, did I scare you?
Did you feel threatened by me?
Did you have to reach for your [ ] ?
cuz I'm [ ] ? Because I told you to not just see
but know I'm [ ] ?

Put it down
Don't be scared
Don't call
Just hear me out
Just listen to
What I have to say.

Don't worry
I'm [ ] armed
I [ ] make a sudden move
I will be [ ].
Just please listen
Don't shoot
I am human just like you

16

Let me breathe
Let me be free
I [ ] harm you
I just want to be heard
I just want you to pay attention.

Okay, did you put your phone down?
Did you put your gun down?
Or do you still feel [ ] by me?

Just hear me out
Won't take too long
I will even have my [ ],
Just listen to me

There is no day
Where I don't have to fear
To go outside
Some fear to go to jail
But us?
We fear [ ].

Our brothers and sisters died
Because our skin made
A threat to your mind

We can't live our lives anymore
We cannot be free
Isn't it ironic
Cuz we live in the land of the "Free?"

You use your Whiteness as a [ ],
Get away with anything

But I can't even [ ] ,
Without getting [ ] and
Do you think you are a hero?
Do you think you can get away with this?
Oh wait. . . . you can
It is I that get lynched
Beat up and criminalized
Because our system is messed up
Just like your goddamn mind

I'M SORRY I'M SORRY
PUT THE GUN DOWN
PLEASE, PLEASE
I HAVE A FAMILY LIKE YOU
I HAVE A DREAM,
THAT I WANT TO COME TRUE
PLEASE DON'T SHOOT
I HAVE MY HANDS UP
DON'T SHOOT
I know you can get away with it
But at least hear me out before you [ ] me

Who knows the other lives,
think about those who didn't get noticed by social media.

It almost seems normal
To see one of us
killed by a [ ] man
It is almost normal
To see a [ ] person
Attack, insult, disrespect us

The news are all about that

kept telling us
"Another Black person died"
"it was *self defense*"
"the killer said he was *scared*"

When will our lives matter?
When will you stop
Taking the lives of dreamers?
Lives of parents?
Lives of children?

I wish I could do more
But I'm out of [ ].
my pain is more than
these couple of words

I can't even live with [ ],
Someone will see me as a threat
cuz of their discomfort

I wish I could walk out free
I wish I could live life without fear
Not thinking about death
Just being me

When will you acknowledge me?
You can see that I'm [ ],
But, I want to live peacefully
Without you fearing that I am a [ ].

Bezawit Abate, who goes by Beza for short, was born and raised
in Addis Ababa, Ethiopia. As a twelve-year-old, she moved to the

United States. She graduated from South High School and is currently studying at Northwestern University as an undergraduate student with the hope of attending medical school. As a child, she developed a love for art. She expressed her emotions and feelings through drawing and poetry. This later developed into a passion for creative writing and painting. Along with those two, she also has a passion for photography and filmmaking. She says "anything art and creativity related, I love it."

America

By Jibril Jama

America is a rough place to live.
America is a tough person to be.

I keep checking the list to see if I'm on it but it seems I'm still on
the waitlist. The longer I'm on it the longer I'm starting to hate this.
When will it be my turn to be an American?

Say one word and you're put in a different label. Feeling like that
new kid that looks in from a different table.

America is a rough place to live.
America is a tough person to be.

I have a lot of love to share and there's a lot of room, everytime I say
assalamu alaikum all they hear is BOOM!

56 hits and Rodney King was on the floor.
After that, you could really hear the roar.

Will I ever fit in? Will it even be right? Will my dreams ever fly high
as a kite?

If I get shot I'll be on the news a couple seconds later I'm yesterday's
news. We're so quick to just change the channel that the story dies,
like a burnt-out candle. Barely 18 years old still learning to rise. I
see the hate in their eyes. The color of my skin is what they despise.

Across the country, there's a lot of movement.
If this is our country there needs to be an improvement.

America is a rough place to live.
America is a tough person to be.

Jibril Jama is a South High School graduate. He is a perceptive writer who likes to write about topics that matter to him. He thinks we should write about stuff that affects our everyday lives.

Light and Dark

By Anonymous

Growing up, my mother was my light. She surrounded my siblings and me with her love, and that was all we needed. I didn't care that there was no food in the fridge. We had each other. There is only one memory I cannot forget. Most I can ignore, pushing them to the deepest parts of my subconscious. For a long time, I chose to forget what that memory was like.

Watching my mother's eyes grow dark, she would wander our apartment listlessly. Sometimes, she would pull me aside and whisper about the people who were watching us, from across the street. But, soon enough, I could hear her humming in the kitchen again with the sweet smell of vanilla pudding calling me to her side. I easily came to accept this as my reality.

Memory is tricky. The line between what is real and what is imagined often blurs. Time twists and shifts my shadowed memories, from who I was as a child to who I am now, obscuring both from view. Thinking back, I can't remember what, or who, came first: the ambulance, or my mother, the phone in her hand, or the sirens in the distance. By borrowing the disjointed stories of my family, I can reconstruct mental images, snapshots in time. My mother standing before me, making a single decision that would change the course of my life.

Over the next year, my siblings and I were shuffled from foster home to foster home, never staying anywhere long. Eventually, in the spring of my first-grade year, we were sent to live with my great-aunt and uncle. My relatives' house was devoid of all warmth. Two no-nonsense people, who had immigrated to the US two decades prior. Both spent the entire day working. Incredibly strict, they would only allow me to go from home to school.

The years passed, each one more unbearable than the next. I realized, quite abruptly, that no matter how I felt, time continued trudging along, past me, taking everyone else along with it. As things stood, I was headed in the same direction as any poor Black kid. Coming from a family of immigrants, I couldn't help but be reminded of all the sacrifices everyone around me had made to get me this far.

It dawned on me that I would probably leave the world exactly as I left it, just as bad as it was before. At that moment, the course of my life was again forever changed because of a single decision. But this time, I made the choice myself. I chose to succeed, and to create a world where no child would have to live the way I had lived, or experience the pain I had felt, ever again. That conviction has carried me to today. When things get too difficult, and I want to give up completely, I always remember this moment, this feeling.

My mother suffered from schizophrenia and PTSD. She did not want to leave us, but she realized it was better than any future we would have with her. She never had a penny to her name, and neither did anyone else in our family. Somehow, she brought us to America. Four months ago, I learned my mother had contracted COVID-19 in her group home. We haven't spoken in so many years, but the thought of never seeing her again destroyed me. Her English is too limited for us to understand each other, but even seeing her was enough to bring so much to the surface.

It took me too long to forgive her, to accept her, and to accept myself. I am her child. I have inherited her pain, and her strength.

Anonymous is a twelfth-grade student at South High School.

A Day in the Life

By Lulya Bereket

I don't think I'm going to be able to look at masks or Zoom the same way ever again. I don't even go outside often, but the frankly horrendous feeling of my own breath slapping me in my face will haunt me like a particularly ambitious ghost for ages. Zoom has an unexpected benefit. I can't be distracted by the kids in the back if there is no classroom to have a back of. Another nice thing about online learning: no one can see or hear me. So as long as I do enough of the work, I can plan world domination and eat fudge in my pajamas. The possibilities are endless. But otherwise? My computer has had so many tabs open for so long it might forget how to completely shut down. My schedule has become like one of those side-quest lists in video games with how weird some of the things I do regularly now are. Though I haven't saved a village from a cartoonishly evil threat, yet. In conclusion, I might be planning world domination. Online learning has been productive. I have learned how to make tasty fudge recently, and I plan to abuse that knowledge for my plentiful nefarious plots in the future.

Lulya Bereket is an eleventh-grade student at South High School. Her favorite colors are gray and blue. She likes to compete to see the maximum amount of time she can spend reading before she has to do her work.

United as One

May we forever stand.
For changing the world
Not letting this pain
Divide us apart
We gotta try to educate every generation about the past
So when the past tries to crawl back
We can take it apart united as one

Haney Mohamed is a former South High student completing her studies at Transition Plus. Haney enjoys writing poetry, making her peers laugh, and imagining better solutions for vision-impaired people.

My Racial Autobiography

By Jibril Jama

Growing up, I thought I needed to tell my story by explaining to people why I was fasting in middle and high school during Ramadan. I felt obliged to do a presentation on Eid in second grade when everyone else was asked to do a presentation on how their families celebrate Christmas. But that has changed. To me, telling my story as a Muslim American has become much less about highlighting what is different about being a Muslim American citizen and more about emphasizing actions that show that Muslims are part of the fabric of America's identity.

When I think of the hardships of being Muslim in America, I think about my parents raising my older siblings during 9/11. I can't imagine raising kids in a country that calls itself the "land of the free" but treats you as if you're a terrorist. When my family moved to Nicollet Ave. to be closer to my dad's job, we were the only Black, Muslim family in our neighborhood. So during the summer, we were hanging out and trying to make friends with the neighbor's kids. One day their parents came to us, and they were talking very slowly and loudly as if we couldn't understand them. They said, "We don't want our kids hanging out with refugees." I've never experienced such a blatantly racist comment. I was honestly stunned and had no response. My little sister was confused about what they said. And so later that night that my parents had to explain that the world is not filled with sunshine and rainbows and that we will run into discrimination a lot in this world. I still get that feeling of being stunned and hearing blatant remarks to this day.

I remember one of my middle school teachers saying something

27

about "your kind" and about violence whenever we talked about 9/11. There were moments like that that shook my foundation, and I also remember always being asked by kids in my class:

"Are you a part of 9/11, or are you ISIS?"

"Did you ever kill anyone?"

"Are you going to bomb this place?"

And they would laugh like it was a joke. But then you ask yourself: How far does a joke go before you say "Is this the only thing you know?"

I remember getting weird looks from strangers when my family and I were going on a trip on a plane. I was scared of flying and my heart was racing so fast I thought it was going to burst out of my chest. My mom could see the look of death on my face, so she told me to read Fatiha from the Quran and to ask God to protect me. So I did what I was told. As I was moving my lips and reading the verses my anxiety improved and I realized it was working, but I could see how people looked uncomfortable and were staring at us. Some lady's kid who was wearing a red Iron Man shirt and had a buzz cut with camouflage shorts came to me and said, "Please don't bomb the plane, I don't wanna die." I thought it was ironic how he was wearing a hero's shirt but was villainizing me and my family. I was honestly stunned my heart wasn't beating fast anymore; in fact it felt like it wasn't beating at all, like everything around me had been frozen. How could he think that I would murder everyone just by practicing my faith?

Reflecting back, I think "Islamophobia" is not really a term that I understood or recognized at the time. How could someone judge someone that they didn't know? But I understood fear, and I understand when people are afraid or fearful they often turn away from and put down what scares them. But once they know better, they do better. So I try to bring whatever information I have, so they can change their beliefs and so that hate can be reduced. I believe there are good Americans who just want to understand. So how do I help them understand? How do I share a meal with my neighbor during the month of Ramadan? How do I, during Eid, give my neighbor's children a dollar or two, or candy, which is what we do when we're celebrating? How do I greet my neighbors, which is a part of Islam? How can I greet them with a smile when they meet me with a grimace? How do I take what I learned from the Quran and the teachings of our prophet, and through my actions and through my behavior help change the views of others? I try to do that every day in small acts. I want to see more peace and not ignorance, so that America can become a place where everyone is truly free and truly welcomed—as they are, without distinction.

Yahweh

By Hawi Emeru

Do you believe in Love?
I do, I believe in the unconditional Love
That has been given to me
To have as well as to share
The Love that saved my life and that made me strong
The Love that gave me a second chance
The Love that helped me forgive others and myself
The Love that unveils the truth to me
The Love that is, was, and will always be pure and just
The Love that builds my brokenness
The Love that holds me together
The Love that will never leave nor forsake me, Yahweh.

Hawi Emeru is a Christian and loves worship music! Hawi likes different forms of art. She is a junior at South High, and her passion is growing in her faith. Hawi enjoys nature and cultural history. Hawi's hobbies are drawing and cooking food. She also enjoys watching anime.

Dominion

By Anonymous

I went to church from the time I was five to the time I was fifteen. Every Sunday I would bow my head in prayer, take communion, and attend Sunday school. The church was beautiful, adorned with huge paintings depicting Christ's crucifixion, the Virgin Mary, and the first communion. Opaque stained-glass windows bathed us in iridescent light.

It was the first Eritrean Eastern Orthodox church in Minnesota. For the few Eritreans living in Minnesota, the importance of having a place to come together cannot be overstated. We are connected by our invisibility; if you are Eritrean, you are family.

Of course, as with any family, there are problems. The church was hierarchical, misogynistic, and homophobic. They shamed anyone who didn't fit their ideals. Because my mother had mental health issues, my reputation was tarnished from the beginning. Attending church was an expectation rather than a choice. Everyone else seemed more connected to Eritrea. I was alone there. I realized it was no longer a place I could thrive. I had to make the decision to leave a part of my culture, a part of myself behind. Beyond what I was expected to become, I needed to find who I could be.

Poem I

Falsify.
Where our bodies end and your flag begins where their land lay and your hands took.
Death.
Practical for us.
Death.
Profit for you.

Gathering.

My breath is deep and heavy pale faces stare at me like I am their reflection.

Hands in my hair like they fishing for something, like they trying to find my spirit, my humanity, ancestry, my soul food, my Nigga, my Negro, my chains, my roots, my "I love you." But your skin a little too dark, too deep, too blue, too ocean, too sun, too moon, too smooth, too jazz, too cotton, too cringe.

But "I love you."

My love so deep I sob at the sight of you, my hands quiver and knees buckle, my love so deep you could drown, you could sink. My shit so deep you can't get out, you can't leave, you can't leave, you can't. Look at you knee on neck suffocating, you deaf, I can't breathe, I can't breathe, you can't breathe. Death. But "I love you."

Scripture beginning, loving, ending. A brown life, a cycle of pain and suffering, a brown life, a cycle of joy and resilience. Let the sky wash over you, let the stars break this generational curse. My God
My mother
My earth
My *everything*.

My love, remember where you came from, you hold the universe within. A star collided with earth and you were born. Trees grew from your fingertips and flowers from your hair. The ocean lay in your womb and the heavens in your eyes. Clay gathered at your feet and roots at your spine.

And it was *beautiful* Black girl.
Beautiful.

Yahanna is a spoken word artist and creative writer. They are a senior at Loring Nicollet Alternative School. Yahanna is passionate about herbalism and holistic healing. They enjoy writing, being in nature, and spending time with family.

The Achilles Heel

By Salma Khalif

As a Black Woman,
We care,
We share,
We love,
We wouldn't even dare to receive.
From the emotional pain and heartache we bare,
To the hatred for us that everyone breeds.
It's okay, Black Women, it's okay.
They see you as strong, they see you as brave.
The shadow behind the hero who doesn't get an ounce of credit
It's expected.
Someone they can spill their thoughts to, full of rotting decay.
It's okay, Black Women, it's okay.
If your counterparts won't protect you,
Then I will.
Let go of the invisible burden on your shoulder
And rest on me.
You are as not as strong as you perceive,
You just had to be.
To survive in a world that wouldn't cater to you.
Be gentle, be weak,
I'll protect you even as you sleep.
Be feminine, be "fleek."
You are "that woman" for most, labeled off as disposable,
You are "my woman" though.
Worth your weight in pearls and gold, just like Beyoncé wrote.

Black Women, we are the blueprint for femininity.

Salma Khalif is a graduate of South High School and is now a freshman at the University of Minnesota majoring in computer science. She's been writing short stories on the side since she was a child with a huge passion for literature. In the next few years, Salma hopes to publish more. She has a huge interest in Multicultural Black Diaspora Literature, which has led to her minoring in Black/ African studies.

My Roots

By Jahanna Osman

Growing up I always felt like I did not fit in, that I would never be the beauty standard since I lived in a predominantly white neighborhood. I had the impression that God had made a mistake. I had the wrong hair, the wrong dead brown eyes, and far too large lips. I have always felt like the odd one out, like the black sheep. In comparison to my white friends, I felt unsightly, and I was always envious of their pin-straight hair and how it slipped out of their hands like a waterfall when you grabbed it, but mine never did. So I started putting relaxer in my hair every third Wednesday of the month. At this point, keratin relaxer had become my best friend; it was the one thing that made me feel pretty enough and valid. Until I was reminded one day that beauty does come in many forms. My trip to Somalia, my hometown, opened my eyes in more ways than I could have imagined. The aroma of Mediterranean spices and gorgeous colorful African tribal designs greeted me everywhere I walked when I first arrived in Mogadishu. Every time I would step foot outside, I would see beautiful Somali women rocking their natural hair and Baatis. The fullness of their lips, the deep, dark brown eyes, and the skin tone that tangoed with the sun still mesmerizes me. As I let my culture consume me, I discovered that beauty flows deep. It's more than just the bright eyes and pin-straight hair. For far too long I've let society dictate my life; it's time to return to my roots. I am beautiful not only because of my physical features but also because I recognize the value of beauty in all cultures. For the first time in my life, I don't feel the need to be envious of other people's beauty since the beauty in myself and my personality is more than enough.

Jahanna Osman is a tenth-grader and self-taught East African author born and raised in Minneapolis, Minnesota. Jahanna grew up with a passion for poetry and writing. Growing up, Jahanna dreamed of becoming a well-known author.

I am

By Haney Mohamed

I am respectful and hesitant
I wonder when people that are in cages will get out.
I hear about world hunger
I see people suffering
I want the world to be peaceful

I am respectful and hesitant
I pretend that I find a way to solve the world's problems.
I feel sad like wilting flowers
SPLASH!!
I am like the ocean so calm and connected
I touch every place
I worry about the Earth
I cry about this generation and the next

I am respectful and hesitant
I understand the world won't stay the same
I say everybody is equal
I dream about visually impaired people having other ways to write
other than technology and Braille
I try to cooperate with Braille and technology
I hope people that have cancer keep on fighting
The way they fight pushes me towards greater things
While I step over a pebble they step over mountains

I am respectful and hesitant

I am a Phoenix
I am
Everlasting

Yellow

By Elsie Carmona Quiterio

If we were all Yellow, God's Peace of color would rain on earth.

Maybe Adam & Eve wouldn't notice they were committing a sin.

If we were all Yellow, maybe Black mothers and fathers and Black children wouldn't be seen as inferior.

Be raped, killed, abused, & enslaved.

If we were all Yellow, would we trust our Police to not judge my skin color? Listen to the tone of my voice? Not discriminate?

If we were all Yellow, would you look at me different because of my age? My size? My clothes that make me colorful? My language?

Would culture exist?

Would race exist?

Would the census exist?

If is the key word.

I shed the blood of my ancestors, hold my weapon; my voice because I am not alone.

The color of my skin does not make me susceptible to your stereotype.

I am a human.

A woman.

I am the master of my multiracial identity.

Dark and light browns nourish my sun, my protection to not shed my pride, I fight.

My eyes are what I see: horror, murder, racial tantrums of the white perspective and worst of all Hate.

The opposite of Love is Fear. Take your Fear and kill it with your melanin Love. Touch, your hands, your healers, your kind.

I am you, melanin brothers and sisters. Hurt from the Pain. My sister, a bullet to the chest, is how the wounds go down 400+ years & layers of blood. I am not indestructible.

We are not bulletproof masses.

When the fight gets too much, we do not get to walk away from the fight. Kiss the wound, give me my hearing.

My wound would hold the next generation because I am not Yellow.

Should I be scared?

The all consuming rotten apple prone to Fear earned the poison and kept losing our people.

We had a moment to become Serenity for a second but then another soul is lost. Supremacy has no room in our unity. In our Earth.

The sun kissed my skin and left my skin to burn in the flames of discrimination & racism.

We need generational help.

Racial Autobiography

By Bianca Morcho

When I was in preschool, we learned colors. We learned about vibrant yellow, mellow blue, fierce red, grassy green, passionate purple, chocolatey brown, and fiery orange. When we talked about shades, we talked about the purest white, the murky gray, and finally, the fear-instilling black. After that lesson, I decided that black was my least favorite color. Black was the color of nightmares that you can't seem to wake up from. Black was the color of fears you couldn't outgrow. Black was the color of death and sorrow. Black was the color of the darkness of abandonment. Any color was better than black. After I learned my colors, I was so excited to show everyone the colors that I now knew. Water was blue, the trees were green, the stop signs were red, and I was brown.

I was telling my friends about my newfound understanding of colors during lunchtime. I pulled my PB&J sandwich out from my little pink backpack and took a big bite before describing the color of everything in sight. To me, the world was so vibrant and colorful and I was glad to be part of it. I was proud to be such a beautiful and earthy color. My skin became something precious to me. The friend who sat closest decided it would be fun to play a game where we guessed what something was based on the given color. I thought I was clever when I said brown—no one would be able to guess it. I revealed the answer because, as I predicted, everyone was stumped. When I told them I was brown, a certain curly-headed friend stopped me.

"You're Black," she said this with pure conviction, as though it were a fact that everyone knew. I insisted that I was brown, not

43

black; I knew I had not learned my colors incorrectly. In winter, my skin was brown like caramel that you put on top of the ice cream that you still eat even when it's snowing outside. In summer, my skin was darkened by the summer like the lucky penny you found on the scorching sidewalk. You see, I knew my colors well. I knew the difference between black and brown, I hadn't confused them. But I didn't tell her this. Instead, I told her to apologize for calling me a color that didn't signify anything good. I would have rather been blue or purple or green. How could I be the color of so many scary things?

"You are Black, and he," as she pointed to our peach-colored friend, "is White." It was very obvious to me at this point that my friend had learned her colors incorrectly. How could our friend possibly be White? He looked like neither paper nor the fluffy snow that was coating the ground. If anything, he was pink and then red when he threw his tantrums. Had she learned her colors incorrectly? Or was I missing something? I moved away from her and sat by myself until it was time to go home.

When I was getting picked up from school, I told my mom what my friend had said. My mom looked at me for a long second before laughing lightly.

"You're right. You are brown," she said with teasing in her voice. I did not understand what her laughing meant then, but I do now.

Now that I'm older, I've had to come to terms with my Blackness. The color black was no longer something I could afford to hate. My status as a Black person was more important than it was when I was a kid. I walk around and the first thing people see about me is my Blackness. I've realized I can't escape from my Blackness, and most recently I've been forced to face it head-on.

George Floyd was murdered by a police officer on May 25, 2020. After his death, it was as if an alarm went off in Minneapolis telling people to take to the streets in protest. Our city looked like that of a warzone for a while. The world was watching our boring little state,

44

and we were all looking for some kind of change. Being forced to acknowledge that "Minnesota nice" is just passive-aggressive racism was one of the biggest epiphanies resulting from the protests. You could see that our city would never be the same. But, along with the protests came a different kind of racism.

Everyone was trying to prove they were not racist. Even celebrities did this, putting on fake tears and raising a fist for Black power while on the inside they were celebrating the fame and publicity they got from "supporting" Black people. Many began using the name of a dead man as a way to gain more fans and support. There were even cases of celebrities taking photos at protests and showing off how much money they donated to Black Lives Matter. There was money to be made from supporting Black people, and many milked it for all it was worth. Some people were walking on eggshells around Black people; these people saw us on the street and their first instinct was to prove they weren't racist or that they supported the "cause." The fires burning on Lake Street were a cool breeze in comparison to the scorching hot gazes of people on the street. Suddenly going on walks became suffocating, and talking to my white neighbors felt patronizing. Sadly, school was not much better. I'd have teachers tell me about how much they love Black people and support the movement (not explicitly, of course). I am still unsure if they were telling me or if they were trying to convince themselves. One of the responses that irritated me was when people would apologize to me and ask if I needed any emotional support. While George Floyd's death was tragic, it shouldn't just be tragic to me because I'm Black. I firmly believe that as a human it should be tragic to see a fellow human die in such a horrible way. It felt like I was expected to give out the mystical "not racist" approval stamp. It was as if we were in court and I somehow became the judge of whether or not the White people I knew were racist or not. Many people were just trying to prevent the destruction of their property, and that meant "appeasing" the Black people.

Looking back, the media was doing their best to ignore the issue of George Floyd's murder and instead focus on the destruction of cities. It was almost as if they wanted to make it look like Black people and other protestors were in the wrong. From that moment on, I realized that as a Black person I would always be looked at negatively even when I was trying to do good. Standing up for myself was overly aggressive, and saying nothing was suspicious or intimidating. And though I had long acknowledged that Black is not a color—if I had kept seeing my Blackness as the color I abhorred as a child—I knew I would come to hate myself.

I had to find new meanings for Black. Black is now the color of the infamous card of limitless spending. Black is now the color of power and social standing. Black is now the color of a mysterious future I have yet to explore. Black is now the color of the elegant black dresses worn by Michelle Obama. Black is now more than the nightmares I feared or the darkness I still cower away from. I now acknowledge that Black is a mixture of all the colors, and while it sometimes may seem grim, there's always something good within its depths.

Bianca Morcho is a graduate of South High School.

Untitled Understanding

By Fredrick Emdin

I've been questioning my lateness but been managing it
I tried to shake off all the trauma but I'm caught in a fix
Vices left from all his madness, wasted time I regret
I know I'll never get a chance to feel and get over it
At night my feelings always shady my chest hollowing in
My sureness and endurance really got caught in a glimpse
Many nights the gangs reacted, bullets fly past the tints
I cannot count how many bombs get released from ha lips

I can see all of the cops, steady, seeking the brown
Tryna sweep up all my people pack em up out my town
The city shady but it's hazy when I leap from my prowl
It's been a while, done stupid shit as a child
But you know better than to go out n' present it so wild
I tried to help but you don't listen and you sit back n' smile
My conscience tell me that you livid so I left for the south
And these are words that spin the world, it's the truth from my mouth
Mountains in my life for views cuz I'on settle with doubt
Momma said I needa listen when the elders around
Pictures painted through the stories for when I hit the ground
It's been a while, I seek the truth through the loud

Let's Make It Great

By Jibril Jama

"Make America Great Again"

What do you mean by that, sir? And by that, I mean at what period of time was America "great?" Was it the period when people who had cinnamon pigment were kept in colonial chains and were the product of the triangular trade? Was it the period of inequality and suffrage for women? Was it the period where people were in anguish due to the economic recession?

It seems to me that America was never great. Stop reaching for something that never was there and focus on making new ambitions. For then America will truly be great.

Human of South High

By Valencia Carlson

This is my American story. My story, a tenth grader ready for an adventure. I am sixteen years old, Black/Haitian, and I have seven siblings. I have moved states three times throughout my whole lifetime: Michigan, Iowa, and Minnesota. I am kind-hearted and a good listener, and I love telling stories and hanging out with my friends. I am athletic and love to stay healthy, which is kind of hard because I love to eat junk food. My favorite chips are Takis. They are so good! I love that they're spicy and I really could eat them every day, but they're bad for your stomach. These are just some of the things that have shaped who I am.

I am the type of girl that loves to do things and talks a lot about something that I really love. I like to babysit and hang out with little kids to get to know them and to see them grow into their own selves. I love to care for others. I also love dogs, talking about dogs and all the different breeds of dogs. I would love to own a dog in the future. For example, I am very energetic, so I love to dance. I can dance almost anywhere and at any time. My favorite music to dance to is Afrobeats.

I would also want to help fight the unequal injustice that is happening in our community and to fight for our equal rights. Being an American has affected different people in many ways. I will tell how it affects me and my family. What I think about being an American has an impact on me and the people around me. Being American is to go through struggles as a whole. It means to not know a lot of your history. It means to have your history be sugarcoated and rooted in white supremacy. Not all our history is taught to us. They teach us the basics of slavery, glorify the founding fathers, and I feel like our history gets taught by people that don't know it or respect it as much as the people that actually have to go through it or experience it. It means having the opportunity to have a better chance of surviving, getting a job, and a house. It means sharing your background and your culture with others and getting to know cultures different from your own. It means having two identities. I think that US history has shaped me and my family.

Black girls get put into a box of a narrative of growing up too soon and being too grown, and we get pushed to the standard of what it means to be "acceptable." We feel pressured to meet other races' expectations, otherwise we won't be accepted. We have to have our hair straightened, talk a certain way, and act a certain way to avoid harmful stereotypes. This is how being American has shaped me and my identity as a Black Woman. White supremacy tells girls like me that we do not have a future and that we are a threat. I feel like us Black women support Black men when it comes to injustice, but when it comes to Black women like Breonna Taylor and all the other women, we don't get the same support and respect that the Black men do. US history as it is communicated relegates my siblings and me to a harder life because of our skin color.

However, the other side of my family, since we were adopted by a white family, will have a better chance of not getting killed simply because they're white. My relatives don't have to deal with the fear of their life maybe being taken from them because of a racist human being. It's very confusing and hard. I only have certain access to what my white family members have. Knowing I will be judged no matter what, my life hasn't ever been the same after coming to that realization. It hurts and makes me sad to know that this judgment isn't just from the outside but from my own family.

Even though things seem fine on the surface, the divide in the US is still real, and it hasn't gone away. We, the younger generation, are still dealing with the same things that our parents had to deal with and our grandparents did. This is a topic not talked about enough, and this needs to change. The future worries me because I don't feel safe or welcome in it. I always feel like you have to be on your toes and stuff. You never know if it's gonna happen to you or if something is gonna happen to you because of your skin color. It makes me sad when I think about how we as Black Women don't have the same support from the community that others have. The Black community is supposed to have our back, but there's a lot of trauma within our community that keeps us from coming together. We need to build a community that's intentional and we need to heal. Honestly, I don't even know how to build or rebuild our community. We see so many movies and stuff that frames us as struggling. I want to see more stories and media of us striving and coming together but in a way that leaves room for our humanity. We are more than our trauma. What I have learned from the Humans of South High (HOSH) project is how other people see me and how I see myself and what it really means to be an American.

To be an American means to have two different sides. You feel pressured to pick between your American side or your ethnic background or racial background. It's kind of weird because I'm Caribbean but I live in America. I have family back home in the Caribbean, but I'm sure we view what it means to be American differently. It makes me wonder what their view of America is and how they view me. Haiti is an impoverished country. During the earthquake, their home was destroyed, and often when I call back home my mother and relatives ask for money. They think we make more money here. You'd be poor here, but in Haiti you'd be rich. It's a hard reality and tells a lot about our history and how our country was made. Even though we were liberated from slavery first, it's still damaged and we don't have many resources. The earthquakes and the president dying impacted Haiti in a way the US couldn't understand. When things break, they don't always get fixed. The US and Haiti are alike in the way that some people have the money to fix things and others don't.

Even though developed countries are richer and often framed as superior, I feel like in Haiti they're happier even if they're poorer. I feel like that goes for any country outside the US. For example, when I visited Puerto Rico, I was welcomed with open arms, a feeling I haven't felt in the US. Imagine what our country could be like if we actually upheld the values of the American Dream? That's my hope. That we can learn to dream together, instead of living a perpetual nightmare.

Valencia Carlson is an eleventh-grade student at South High School.

What the Stars Said to Humans on Earth

By Bezawit Abate

Inspired by Clint Smith's "what the ocean said to the black boy"

We are only seen in the night sky
disappearing in the daylight
Sun covering our lights
But we come back during the night
shining really bright.

We might look different
shapes
from big to small
Varying from the colors
Red,
Blue,
White.

But you need to know
we are beauty for the sky
bringing light
for the dark night
showing ourselves and our colors
working together
for this night sky.

But you?

What did you do
with your beauty?
What did you do
for your night sky?
Did you work together,
to change the day into the night?

You're just tearing the sky apart
destroying one another
dissolving the night sky away
submitting to the darkness
in exchange for your light.

Because

By Hawi Emeru

I AM going to bring happiness wherever I go
Not because I am lucky
Not because I was born with a unique talent
But because I choose to bring happiness to the places I go to.
I have been hurt by the person that was supposed to show me love
I know how it feels to be left alone
I know how it feels to be misunderstood,
Stuck in a uncomfortable situation I didn't create
To be blamed for the Actions of someone else
To get disgusted looks for standing up in what I believe in,
To be hated for having a voice,
To feel alone even when surrounded by loved ones. I refuse to let the
world crush my spirit.
I will fight not just for Myself but for those who are struggling.
YOU are Not Alone.
Because I AM here . . . Fighting every day just like you.
I'm going to bring happiness wherever I go.

Wet Paint

By Anonymous

Every time I stand in front of a canvas, I am alone. I hold my brush in my hand, softly daubing smooth layers of paint, building each stroke onto the next. For me, art is a celebration of the diversity of life and the connections we experience throughout history. Across communities, cultures, and countries, it is a universal language that connects us. A painting depicts a single moment in the artist's life. You see what the artist feels is important enough to share with the world. There is something so powerful about the ability to express yourself, to be stripped of all ornamentation, and for me, that self-expression allows me to be free.

Painting is the only aspect of my life where there are no limits. I am bound only by my imagination and creativity. What is beautiful, what is evil, what is beginning, what is ending. Art allows me to constantly explore who I am. As I continue to grow, so does my understanding of art. By exploring what art means to me, it expands my view of the world and allows me the freedom to express myself in new and diverse ways.

What's Valid Anymore?

By Salma Khalif

What if I told you I have one of the worst and best combinations of identities there are in this wretched society? This identity which I was born into and am told to protect 'til I'm dead without no reward? What if I told you this identity comes with obstacles and questions that even I myself will never be able to answer? How others will hate me for just having this identity and they don't even know why?

They were told to, so they ran with it. Never questioning it.

Someone chose out of all these combinations of unique identities where they rank. I find myself asking, "Why is one better than the others? Why do seven billion people even accept such a concept?" It's like language. It's only there to aid us in communication. So why? You'd think we'd learn to embrace our differences instead of demonizing them. I believe if we had done that instead maybe we wouldn't have to be martyred and immortalized with a hashtag. Instead of focusing on how they lived, we only focus on how they died. We criminalize the victim before their blood runs cold. But my dehumanization was a life and a death sentence the second you decided not to see me.

My own identity right now in this twenty-first century Western American context is not seen well. I identify as a Black Muslim Woman. Being one of them would've been enough for one person, but I ended up winning the lottery, I guess—one that no one would scratch for. When I go out, I'll have to roll the dice on what I'll be attacked for on any given day. Was it being Black? Or a woman? No, for sure being Muslim, today. It's a fun game to play when you're perceived as a threat to America. Ironically, I have power by being

57

the most powerless person there is. A pro of holding my identity would be the ability to see everyone's true colors. When people view you as less than or disposable, they are more likely to act like their true selves. That is, until we started recording the truth. For all the world to see. You see all types of people and where they stand. It's an advantage like no other and I love having this honor.

So tell me . . .

Is your identity valid?

A Poem and a Letter to America

By Yahanna

Sometimes I think it's the end. For a moment I find myself in peace, until I see the news—another Black man dead, and I'm reminded of our reality. How many more Black bodies will it take to please you? How many more live lynchings, traffic stop executions, brutal beatings, cries for mothers—I can't breathe, I can't breathe. How many more times does our city have to burn? How many communities destroyed? Emmett Till because he whistled. Tamir Rice for being a child. Atatiana Jefferson, "wrong place, wrong time."

How many more lives lost?

So much White Silence and Minnesota Nice, performative posts and meaningless signs. Like we aren't dying. Like this ain't the equivalent to being hanged from a tree with everyone watching. Like cops weren't created to catch and kill. Like this is just a one-time thing and not genocide. Like this system is broken when it works the way it's supposed to. And it works the way it's supposed to. So what will you say, what will you do when this all comes back to you? When truth comes knocking at your door? When it's time to answer for all crimes committed? All the children you took? What will you say on your day of reckoning? I'm sorry?

Where is my Humanity. Where is my Humanity? You have stolen it from me and from all of mine.

On Sunday April 11, Daunte Wright was murdered at the hands of a police officer in the name of Racism. In the name of Hatred. There is no need for further circumstance. The good or bad he's done is irrelevant to his death. His life being taken. To justify a murder or to bestow "martyr" onto someone is to dehumanize them. Daunte lived. That's what matters.

He lived.

In these times it is so important for us to actively rest, to love on ourselves, to radically dream for our communities and the ones we lost. And remember,

We Will Breathe.

Pressure

By Fredrick Emdin

My chest is hurting
An unfamiliar sensation
Disappearing smoke puffin suffering from inhalation
Been isolated from myself I'm non-loving
Using up my time distracted from my vision
What's my flight? What's the point of a summer with no plight?
Speeding down Hiawatha with the boys every night
Bleeding from the nose as I tried facing my frights
Cried
inside my dreams seeing sight I'm like a damn kite
Look up out my blinds every time I see what life is like
No time wasting for opinions on the daily
Walk back and forth till my soul got lazy
Made more sense than a dollar, you can't chain me
Change me, portray me as a dog, I got rabies
Portray me as a demon in your doorway
Ya heart falls onto the floor looking all crazy
Ya soul got snatched out ya clothes, a walking zombie
Workhorse, lab rats, nigga we all sheep
Listen to my ghost stories every time I sleep
Cruisin with my forefathers nigga shit is deep
Fished out my problems when the cold came in
Lost growth from most of my pain that's within

For the Innocent Ones

By Bezawit Abate

For those who lost their lives
treated inequitably
misjudged for their
culture, religion,
tribe, identity

For those who lost family
who felt powerless
and trapped

For those threatened,
told they would die
the next day

For those whose bodies
were thrown away like nothing,
Murdered

For those who were forced
to take off their crosses
Forced to disown their religion

For those who stayed
and surrounded the church
to keep it from
burning down

For those who were
targeted by avaricious people

For the kid who had to
walk through war
just to get his education
with a broken heart
and face full of sadness

For those whose lives were
altered by this whole mess
a better day will come
we survived once
and we will survive again

We survived Yodit Gudit
We can survive this plague
Of killing each other
For race, tribe, and religion.

We must join hands
And work together
To seek the light.

Let's not shed hopeless tears
Let's stand side by side
Let's defeat our enemies
Defeat those who wish not to see peace in their country.

Let's create a better life
By making our motherland a place for everyone
Let's bring peace to one another
Respect innocent ones and love each other.

Bloom

By Elsie Carmona Quiterio

One day I'll write about the flowers like we own them.

Their delicacy has been touched by rough hands, their grave has been deflowered, their beauty has been dismissed in petals.

You walk in my garden and murder my plants?

How dare you dehydrate my youth to tend to and water your weeds?

Have I told you I have been touched? I have been bruised with fingers in places where the sun doesn't shine? See the sun hides those places to protect.

Don't fall for the rose and forget it has thorns.

I am not the colonizer. I am being killed by your fertilizer. Your chemicals. Your sins. Your anger.
I am weak.

I try to make love to my sun but I am gone.

Nurture my garden when I am gone for I am legendary.

The flower who cried thorns.

Spring Growth

By Haney Mohamed

New possibilities
Colorful birds migrating back
The scent of hope in the air

Breath in Memory of . . .

By Yahanna

A eulogy to every human that's been executed
In the name of racism.
In the name of hate.
You have been and done so much.
Carried your joy even while being brutalized and
Burdened with their illness.
There was no reason for your death.
The earth misses your step.
The sky misses your smile.
The air misses your cry.
The stars miss your laugh.
The moon misses your sob.
The sun misses your soul.
They miss you, we all do.

An Energy Breath to all who continue to live
While experiencing suffering,
As you read
Breathe deeply,
My love, this is a continuation
Of your life,
You are living, here, now,
Being,
Voices may ask you, is that enough?
Yes my love,

You are enough,
Your existence was always enough,

Remember where you came from,
A star collided with earth and you were born,
You hold the power of healing within,
I know you feel alone,
Like no one hears your hurt,
But remember where you come from,
Community,
I gotchu my love,
We all do <3

Letter of Gratitude for the Writers of *Rehumanize Me*

The book in your hands is a testament to the times we're in. It also reflects the impossibility of ignoring our truths and the power of our voices. The writers you have just read in this book were born to create, as I believe you were. I hope their words have inspired you toward this truth: There is no option to be silent, especially now.

I sat by the sea, recently, with a copy of Octavia Butler's *Parable of the Sower* and came across the famous life-shaping quote that has affected the writing of so many creators through time:

"All that you touch, you change. All that you change changes you ... God is Change."

The writers of this incredible body of work have held the tension of growing and thriving in a pandemic, and an uprising that followed the untimely death of George Floyd, with Daunte Wright's death not too far behind. They've endured a contentious swirl of political mayhem while studying, working, writing, and living in a city struggling to find, fix, and heal itself. As I read their words, I couldn't help but feel the balm seep into my unsettled psyche, and the same emotions surfaced reading Ms. Butler's words. I've searched for healing and the writings of our soothsayers to guide me through these times. *Rehumanize Me* is a book I couldn't have predicted would be precisely what I needed—prophetic, prescient, and a mirror reflecting back at me the Change I hope is near. The power of truth. The power of voice.

The God in Octavia Butler's Parables series—the Master of Change—has become a sort of new Mother for me. Octavia's God is invested most in movement, in an ever-flowing, constant shift. In this moment, Change unapologetically beckons me, beckons all of us, to lean into adaptability when we feel most rigid, loathe safety, and push for a world where we are all seen. Vulnerability is where we find the actual ammunition to free us. The writers of *Rehumanize Me* are writing from this space, and I can't thank them enough for leaning into their own vulnerability—it's truly a gift and a map.

"All that you touch You Change. All that you Change Changes you . . . God is Change."

Thank you to these writers who persisted through moments of crippling volatility in the world for birthing new, old, and neo-revolutionary words. Thank you for persisting through the same apathy and complacency of Maya's White supremacist America, and Phyllis's, and Nikki's, and Richard's, and Marcus's, and W.E.B.'s. Thank you for persisting in writing truths that had not been written quite like how you have written them. Thank you for enduring through the same and old and new tears, scars, wounds, and nightmares as our ancestors and for birthing another new story that will carry us back to ourselves and forward into a future where we are humanized again. Your perspectives in *Rehumanize Me* will stretch you and us. Your questions will shake us awake with a renewed inflection and break us open again. The urgency of now punches through these pages unapologetically.

When I imagined Project Exodus as a reparations program that would center the voices of Black writers creating projects like *Rehumanize Me*, it was because the written word saved my life. Black writers were and have always been my North Star to liberation. And so, thank you to the *Rehumanize Me* authors for answering the call to write and for choosing to do it now. It's not an easy time to be a writer, especially a young Black writer, a champion of Revolution, praying at the altar of Change. It's never easy to see the signs—injustices, brokenness, glitches—that the masses have allowed to atrophy in their imaginations and to settle like dust in their memories. It's even more challenging to write them as true yet again.

I'm honored to have played a small part in this project. Dear

Rehumanize Me writers, you have indeed scribed a tune that tomorrow's freedom fighters will hum to.

Sincerely,

Dara Beevas
CEO of Wise Ink Creative Publishing
Founder of Project Exodus
Author of the Li'l Queens Children's Picture Book Series

Educator Resources

Rehumanize Me is a book project unlike any we've done in the past for a multitude of reasons. For starters, *Rehumanize Me* is part of Wise Ink's Project Exodus program and 826 MSP's Young Authors' Book Project program.

Project Exodus is "a cultural reparations program for Black storytellers, artists, creatives, community organizers, and activists who are on the frontlines of helping heal our community. Each book serves as a bridge to healing for Black and Brown communities and education for the general community while also being a financial vehicle for an author to reinvest in future projects if they choose to."

In the Young Author's Book Project (YABP), educators, volunteers, and staff work together to support students in the creative process of writing original works around a theme. Illustrators, designers, publishers, and printers collaborate with students and classroom volunteers to create a professionally published anthology each school year.

For the first time with this year's YABP, rather than working with a class or group of classes at a particular school, we formed a Student Editorial Board to lead the project from across multiple Minneapolis high schools. This created a wider literary arts community for our young authors, as they built connections with other young Black writers as well as adult mentors.

The words of the young authors published in this book speak powerful truths. After the murder of George Floyd and the Uprising which began in our home neighborhood of South Minneapolis, we knew that the wider community needed to hear from Black youth more than ever before.

As the title suggests, the writing in this book conveys a wide scope of students' experiences. Themes include liberation, healing, identity, Black Joy, and so much more. To quote author and Editorial

Board member Yahanna, "We're not just a movement. We're humans that have lives."

This project was led by an editorial board of seven Black youth from Minneapolis. After applying and being selected to join the board, these students (ages 15–18) developed submission guidelines, promoted the opportunity to peers, submitted and edited their own writing, edited writing from peers, and then made final decisions on the design and professional aesthetic of the publication. Additionally, seven other young writers submitted pieces which were selected for final publication. This array of youth includes diverse representation across the African diaspora—including immigrant and mixed-race Black youth, Queer Black folx, and those with disabilities.

As such, the educator resources are very different from previous projects. Instead of heavily teased out writing activities and modeling explicit writing styles, we let the Editorial Board members' creative spirits flow and supplemented their creativity with a series of writing prompts, intentional conversations, and community building. As with many projects that took place during the COVID-19 pandemic, the majority of our meetings were virtual. Thus, in recognition of Zoom burnout, pandemic fatigue, and the Derek Chauvin trial for the murder of George Floyd, we as a team had to be flexible, constantly pivot, and leave room for grace. These prompts and the spoken word lesson reflect those challenges and triumphs we navigated over the course of distance learning last year. All of our sessions consisted of a check-in question to elicit conversation around emotions or imagination, as well as a writing prompt. The consistency of this practice and the focus on the students' topics of interest allowed us to build a strong bond of community, even when most of our interactions were through screens. Staff participated in the conversations and writing just as the students did, which demonstrated a reciprocal trust and transparency that encouraged more active student participation.

Spoken Word Lesson

One session, one hour (could be extended over longer multiple sessions if necessary)

- Brief check-in (refer to Discussion Starters/Community Builders below)

- Have students listen to reading of "Summer of 2009" by Hanif Abdurraqib, which can be found on YouTube via Button Poetry. (5 mins)

- Have students annotate and highlight the piece as you either listen to it a second time or read it out. (5 mins)

- Have students share their findings with the class. (5 mins)

- Have students read popcorn style the poem "Fuck Your Lecture on Craft, My People Are Dying" by Noor Hindi, which can be found online in the Poetry Foundation's archive, and repeat the annotating and share-out process. (15 mins)

- Use these writing stems for the writing activity so students can create their own! (30 mins)

- "It is summer of 2020_____"

- "One day, I'll write about the flowers like we own them__"

- Closing

Additional Resources

Writing Stems

- I remember ...

- In memorial of ...

Writing Prompts

- What is your favorite part of your identity?

- Would you rather go to the past to meet your ancestors? Or go to the future to meet your descendants?

- What is your favorite childhood meal?

- What is one self-care act/activity you practice regularly and why?

Discussion Starters/ Community Builders

- What issues are coming up on your feed?

- What issues are close to your heart?

- What do you think folks need to hear from Black Diasporic Youth?

- What qualities/tools do you need to succeed in a group setting?

- What has your healing journey been like? (individually)

- What does healing look like in your family, neighborhood, school, or community?

- What or who has been helpful in your healing journey?

About 826 MSP

826 MSP is a nonprofit youth writing center that empowers under-served Twin Cities students in grades K-12 to think creatively, write effectively, and succeed academically alongside a community of caring volunteers. The organization was founded in 2009 in response to Minnesota's opportunity gap, and continues to work toward ending inequities by amplifying student voice. Our youth writing center, located in South Minneapolis, provides a safe, welcoming creative space. We sincerely believe that a fun, beautiful space helps to inspire, cultivate, and broadcast students' creativity.

In 2019, 826 MSP became the ninth chapter of 826 National, a network of youth writing and tutoring centers in major cities throughout the United States. 826 National's philosophy is that individualized attention is critical to improving literacy and equipping students for success. We work toward our mission and serve our community through the following programs:

After-School Writing Lab: This program serves about sixty students per semester in grades K–12. Four days a week, trained volunteer tutors provide academic support and creative writing activities. Creative writing by the young authors of ASWL is published through chapbooks and celebrated with community release parties twice annually.

Storytelling and Bookmaking Field Trips: Available to second-through fifth-grade public school classes across the Twin Cities, our field trips strive to embolden our next generation of writers to explore and value their own voice. Students and teachers join us to craft original narratives as a class. Volunteers, including an illustrator, work with student authors to publish a book within three hours.

Writers' Room: 826 MSP works in concert with the staff and students at South High School to create a drop-in satellite writing center within the school to support students and teachers for all their writing needs. For teachers, this includes lesson plan support and project ideas, and for students, this includes help with college essay writing, homework assignments, and even personal writing projects.

Creative Writing Workshops: Held periodically for a variety of ages and interests, each workshop represents a collaboration between student authors, volunteers, and community partners working to create original pieces around a theme.

Young Authors' Book Project: Classroom teachers, volunteers, and 826 MSP staff work together to support students in the creative process of writing original works around a theme. Illustrators, designers, publishers, and printers collaborate with students to create a professionally published anthology of their work.

Young Authors' Council: 826 MSP's newest youth leadership programs connects youth through writing and civic engagement. Each school year, the program offers fifteen youth a paid fellowship, publishing opportunities, and leadership experience. YAC is open to students in grades 7–12 who attend Twin Cities metro schools.

About Project Exodus

Project Exodus is a cultural reparations program under Wise Ink's Our Own Voices initiative for Black storytellers, artists, creatives, community organizers, and activists who are on the frontlines of helping heal our community. This annual program funds ten recipients' book projects 100 percent. The recipients retain 100 percent ownership and also 100 percent profit. Two of the projects are helmed by recipients under eighteen; one of these is *Rehumanize Me*. Each book serves as a bridge to healing for Black and brown communities and education for the general community while also being a financial vehicle for an author to reinvest in future projects if they choose to.

About the Illustrator

Myc Dazzle a.k.a. Daz is a strategist, illustrator, and storyteller. He is the founder of creative agency Discover Dope Creative and co-founder of edtech startup Schoolz. He is a polymath and problem solver with a passion for all things creative. Doing things right (i.e. efficiently, enthusiastically, and comprehensively) is an idea that permeates every aspect of Daz's work.

Acknowledgments

From its inception, *Rehumanize Me* was a team effort made joyous and excellent by the many hands who brought it to life. We would like to acknowledge and sincerely thank everyone who made this beautiful anthology possible:

To our school staff liaison and counselor Farah Hussein, whose kind and gentle leadership helped build a community of trust and care with our editorial board.

To all our volunteers who help 826 MSP deliver our free programs, but especially to the late Paul Von Drasek. With self-deprecating humor and infinite patience, Paul was the Young Authors' Book Project's biggest champion—both in and out of the classroom. We miss his encouraging words and gentle prodding that brought the past five YABPs to fruition. We are eternally grateful to Paul's wife, Lisa Von Drasek, and all their friends and family who continue to support 826 MSP.

To 826 MSP's staff, including Samantha Sencer-Mura, Ashley Lustig, Cristeta Boarini, Ellen Fee, Jeannine Erickson, and Aminah Hussein, who exemplify a student-centered vision in all they do: from grant writing to hosting a movie night and all the fun and not-so-fun duties in between. Every writing conference or parent phone call you made helped this book make it to the finish line.

To brilliant teaching artist Keno Evol, who brought inspiring conversation and writing prompts to our students and showed them how a published writer and community-driven leader could look and talk like them.

To our illustrator Myc Dazzle, who brought whimsy and vivacity into the stunning drawings that grace these pages. Through tireless rounds of edits, you turned the students' doodles and marginalia into the personification of Black joy.

To Wise Ink Creative Publishing, especially Dara Beevas and Alyssa Bluhm. After six YABPs together, this partnership continues to grow stronger with every passing year. Such wonderful publications have only been possible thanks to your warm guidance and commitment to excellence. We're honored to be on your team.

To 826 MSP's committed and visionary board of directors, and the community that continues to support us, especially the Friends of South High Foundation, the Beim Foundation, the Mithun Family Foundation, 826 National, the Cuttlefish Society, the Morning Foundation, the Minneapolis Foundation, the ECMC Foundation, the Walser Foundation, the Hawkins Project, and our Kickstarter backers. Your support ensures our students' meaningful words can make their way into the world.

This work is funded in part by the Minnesota Humanities Center with money from the Arts and Cultural Heritage Fund that was created with the vote of the people of Minnesota on November 4, 2008. Additionally, this activity is made possible by the voters of Minnesota through a Minnesota State Arts Board Operating Support grant, thanks to a legislative appropriation from the Arts and Cultural Heritage Fund.

CLEAN WATER LAND & LEGACY AMENDMENT

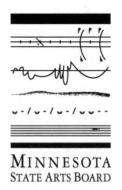

MINNESOTA STATE ARTS BOARD

Land Acknowledgment

Today, eleven tribal nations and communities are located within the state of Minnesota—the place 826 MSP calls home. 826 MSP pays tribute to the Dakota and Ojibwe as the original people of this sacred land, first called Mni Sota Makoce in the Dakota language.

Mni Sota Makoce is a place that carries a deep, layered history across the thousands of years the Dakota and Ojibwe peoples have been in kinship with the land, and in the centuries since European settlers colonized the land that the state of Minnesota now occupies. The land seizures and genocide commited by the United States were projects of spiritual and cultural destruction that denied the Dakota free and unhindered access to the land that fundamentally shapes their identity. We acknowledge that trauma has occurred, that harm continues to occur today, and that it is incumbent upon all of us residing on this land to work toward an equitable future where everyone has the opportunity to thrive. We encourage you too to learn and consider the history of the land on which you reside, as well as the resilient peoples and complex legacies that have made it what it is today.

Student Editorial Board

SALMA KHALIF

YAHANNA

HAWI EMERU

ELSIE CARMONA
QUITERIO

FREDRICK EMDIN

BEZAWIT ABATE

HANEY MOHAMED